FANTASTIC FIGURES!

The Math of **Shapes**

Written by Bill Harrod

WORLD BOOK

www.worldbook.com

Co-published by agreement between Shi Tu Hui and World Book, Inc.

Shi Tu Hui
Room 1807, Block 1,
#3 West Dawang Road
Chaoyang District, Beijing 100025
P.R. China

World Book, Inc.
180 North LaSalle Street
Suite 900
Chicago, Illinois 60601
USA

© 2026. All rights reserved. This volume may not be reproduced in whole or in part in any form without prior written permission from the publisher.

WORLD BOOK and the GLOBE DEVICE are registered trademarks or trademarks of World Book, Inc.

Library of Congress Control Number: 2025942225

Aha! Academy: Math
ISBN: 978-0-7166-7377-4 (set, hardcover)

Fantastic Figures! The Math of Shapes
ISBN: 978-0-7166-7383-5 (hard cover)
ISBN: 978-0-7166-7446-7 (e-book)
ISBN: 978-0-7166-7436-8 (soft cover)

Staff

Editorial

Vice President
Tom Evans

Editorial Project Coordinator
Kaile Kilner

Senior Curriculum Designer
Caroline Davidson

Curriculum Designer
Mikayla Kightlinger

Proofreader
Nathalie Strassheim

Indexer
Nathaniel Lindstrom

Graphics and Design

Senior Visual Communications Designer
Melanie Bender

Designer
Shannon Hagman

Written by Bill Harrod

Designed by Starletta Polster

Acknowledgments

The publishers gratefully acknowledge the following sources for photography. All illustrations were prepared by WORLD BOOK unless otherwise noted.

Cover: Dirk Ercken/Shutterstock; lzf/Shutterstock; Laborant/Shutterstock Unleashed Design/Shutterstock; Vera Larina/Shutterstock

© Bernie Nunez, Getty Images 15; NASA 5, 39, 40, 43; Public Domain 23; © Shutterstock 4, 5, 6, 7, 8, 9, 10, 11, 12, 13, 14, 15, 16, 17, 18, 19, 20, 21, 22, 23, 24, 25, 26, 27, 28, 29, 30, 31, 32, 33, 34, 35, 36, 37, 38, 39, 40, 41, 42, 43, 44, 45, 46, 47, 48; NASA/JPL/USGS 43

There is a glossary of terms on page 48. Terms defined in the glossary are in type that looks like *this* on their first appearance on any spread (two facing pages).

Contents

Introduction 4

① **Shapes around us** 6
    Hello, my name is 8
    Circles and their curved friends 10
    Shapes at the store .12
    Shapes at play 14

② **Shapes in nature** 16
    Animals using math .18
    Stripes and spots 20
    Elaborate patterns 22
    Triangular trees and fractal ferns 24
    Rainbows 26

③ **Shapes in structures** .28
    Build like an Egyptian 30
    Ancient architecture .32
    The mighty triangle! .34
    Contemporary construction 36

④ **Shapes in space** 38
    Ducks in space? 40
    Planets on the move .42

The power of the cylinder! 44
Index 46
Glossary 48

Introduction

When you look at the world around you (and the worlds beyond), you see beautiful shapes everywhere. And not just the familiar *shapes* you learn about in school!

You may not realize it, but, in the background, math often guides why things are shaped the way they are. Shapes help animals eat ... and avoid being eaten! Shapes help plants grow, structures stay up, and the universe stay in motion.

Learn why Earth is shaped the way it is and moves the way it does.

Knowing the math behind the shapes can help you understand why the world functions like it does. Maybe you will find uses for these different shapes in your own lives! Join us as we look at shapes and the math that makes them.

I don't like the looks of that cheetah on the other page!

SHAPES AROUND US

Let's start at the very beginning … a very good place to start! All *shapes* have names. No, not names like "Mike" or "Barb." But names that tell us a little about the shape's look and properties.

Some shapes are made up of straight lines and others have curves. Some are even in 3D! While you are probably familiar with some of their names, others will be new to you.

I love circles! Tell me more!

Some shapes often have special properties or characteristics. For example, circles have a special property that your dog might enjoy. Other curved shapes describe the path of planets around the sun, baseballs hit by your friends, and cannonballs shot by your enemies. Shapes are also important in the games you play and at the grocery store where you shop.

So, read on, as we begin to learn about shapes and their uses!

Shapes around us

Hello, my name is....

You are probably familiar with many types of polygons, including triangles, rectangles, squares, hexagons, and octagons. These shapes are seen in buildings, nature, space, and elsewhere. Read on to see where and why.

Shapes are generally named based on how many sides they have. Some well-known polygons are:

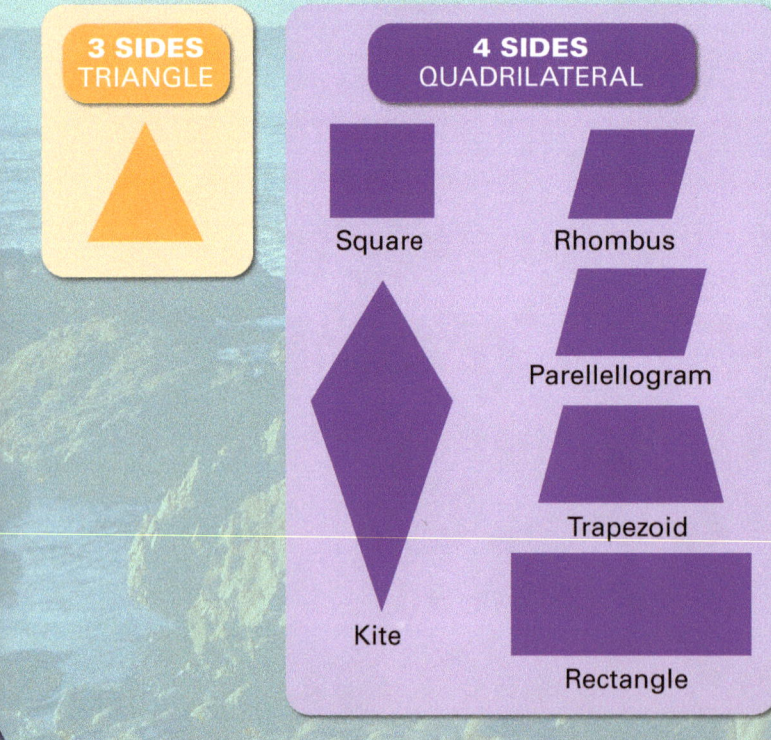

- **3 SIDES** TRIANGLE
- **4 SIDES** QUADRILATERAL: Square, Rhombus, Parellellogram, Trapezoid, Kite, Rectangle
- **5 SIDES** PENTAGON
- **6 SIDES** HEXAGON
- **8 SIDES** OCTAGON
- **10 SIDES** DECAGON

A soccer ball is made up of 12 black pentagons and 20 white hexagons.

8

Let's start by looking at *polygons*. Polygons are closed, flat *shapes* whose sides are straight lines. Even though such shapes as circles (not made up of straight lines) and *cubes* (not a flat shape) are NOT polygons, we will look at them later on.

The Giant's Causeway is an unusual formation of rock columns along Northern Ireland's north coast. According to legend, the causeway was built as a bridge for giants passing between Ireland and Scotland.

Kites, parallelograms, rectangles, rhombuses, squares, and *trapezoids* are all types of quadrilaterals. This brick wall is made up of a bunch of quadrilaterals.

A, **C**, and **F** are trapezoids.
B and **E** are parallelograms.
D is a rhombus (special parallelogram).

DID YOU KNOW?

Do you know what we call a figure with 127 sides? Neither do we! So, we will just call it a 127-gon. It's OK to name polygons with a large number of sides like that.

Shapes around us

Circles and their curved friends

One use of circles is in the wheel. Wheels on bikes, cars, and many other vehicles are circular because circular wheels have less friction and give a smoother ride than what you would get from wheels of other *shapes*. Can you imagine the problems you would have riding a bike with square- or other-shaped wheels?

No fence can hold me!

Compared to other shapes, circles enclose the largest *area* for a given perimeter. What does that mean? Let's say that you are given some wood to build a fence for your dog to play in. The largest fence (area-wise) that you could build would be shaped like a circle.

Most of the shapes that you are used to have straight lines. Some figures have curved sides. Let's look at circles and other curved figures.

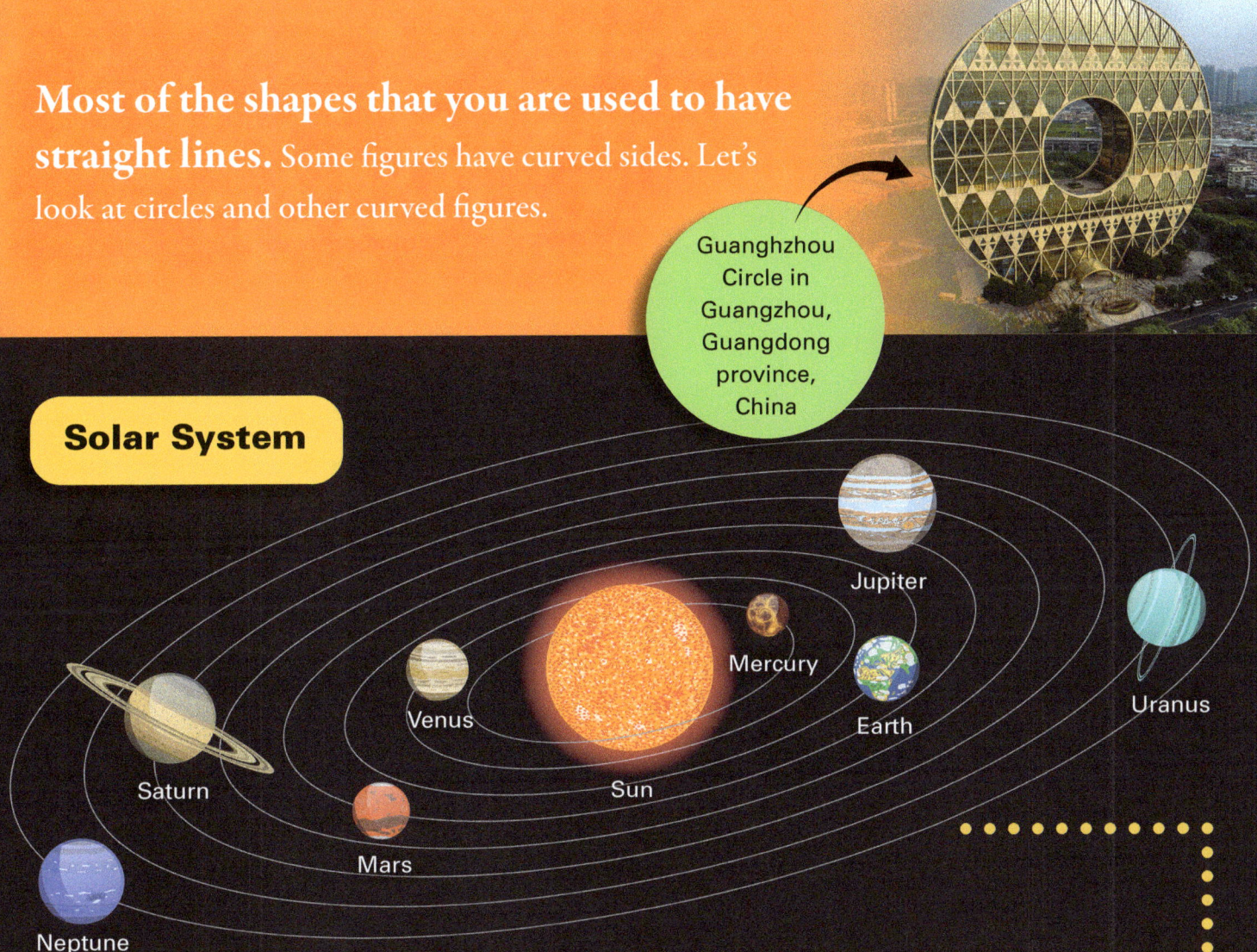

Guanghzhou Circle in Guangzhou, Guangdong province, China

Solar System

One special type of curve is a type of oval called an *ellipse*. Many people think that Earth *orbits* the sun in a circle, but Earth and other planets actually orbit the sun in an ellipse.

Another special type of curve is the *parabola*. Parabolas describe the motion of such objects as a baseball or cannonball. So, if you want to know where to stand to catch a flyball (or, where not to stand if you want to avoid getting hit by a cannonball), parabolas are your friends.

Shapes around us

Shapes at the store

Next time you are at the grocery store, look at the cans for soup, soda, vegetables, and many other products. You might notice all the cans are in a special shape called a *cylinder*. But why this shape? A cylinder uses less metal (and is, therefore, cheaper) to make then if you made a differently shaped can that held the same amount of food or drink.

Have you ever tried to crush an empty soda can? (Be careful if you do because the can will get jagged edges when you crush it. Might be better to use your shoes!) It is almost impossible to crush the can unless you put a dent in it first—then it is rather easy. This may seem unimportant now, but, later on, we will see a connection with soda cans and the Parthenon in Greece!

We've learned about some different *shapes.*
Let's head to the local grocery store and see some of these shapes in action!

After you are done looking at the cans, go to the cereal aisle. What shape do you notice? Cereal, and many other foods in the grocery store, for that matter, have boxes that are in a shape called a rectangular *prism.* But why? Boxes of this shape can be stacked close together, which minimizes unused shelf space. They are also easy to store and ship.

DID YOU KNOW?

Want to find an easy way to stack watermelons? Grow them in *cubes!* They stack nicely and they taste the same as normal watermelons.

Shapes around us

Shapes at play

Have you ever played chess or checkers? These games are played on a square board that has 8 rows of 8 squares each, for a total of 64 squares. Here are some other games:

Tic-tac-toe	3 rows of 3 squares each = **9 squares**
Bingo	5 rows of 5 squares each = **25 squares**
Sudoku	9 rows of 9 squares each = **81 squares**

Do the numbers 9, 25, 64, and 81 look familiar to you? Those are *square numbers*. Do you now see why we call these special numbers "square numbers"?

X	1	2	3	4	5	6	7	8	9	10
1	1	2	3	4	5	6	7	8	9	10
2	2	4	6	8	10	12	14	16	18	20
3	3	6	9	12	15	18	21	24	27	30
4	4	8	12	16	20	24	28	32	36	40
5	5	10	15	20	25	30	35	40	45	50
6	6	12	18	24	30	36	42	48	54	60
7	7	14	21	28	35	42	49	56	63	70
8	8	16	24	32	40	48	56	64	72	80
9	9	18	27	36	45	54	63	72	81	90
10	10	20	30	40	50	60	70	80	90	100

Without realizing it, you have probably played many games in which shapes are important. Let's specifically look at a few games whose boards are squares.

Square roots are a bit like the opposite of square numbers. You can use **square roots** to find the size and **dimensions** of a game board. For example, a Battleship game board has 100 squares. What number multiplied by itself (or what number squared) gives a product of 100? 10! So we can say people play Battleship on a 10x10 grid.

The game of Go is played on a board that has lines (some going across, some going down) that form a square grid with 361 *intersections*. Because the square root of 361 is 19, we can find that Go is played on a grid with 19 lines across and 19 lines down.

TECH TIME

Computers have been programmed to win at chess and Go! In 1997, a computer, called Deep Blue, defeated chess world champion Garry Kasparov in a six-game series (3 ½ - 2 ½). In 2016, a computer program named AlphaGo defeated Go grandmaster Lee Sedol in a five-game series (4-1).

Garry Kasparov in his 1997 chess match against Deep Blue

SHAPES IN NATURE

While we are pretty sure that animals don't actually go to school to study math, some animals do use *shapes* and their mathematical properties! For example, animals can build structures whose specific shape increases their effectiveness. Have you ever noticed the designs that some animals have on their bodies? These colorful designs aren't just for looks. In some cases, these designs can help animals survive!

As you spend time outdoors, you see that nature has beauty all around it. Let's see how shapes contribute to the beautiful world of nature!

Not only am I good-looking, but my colorful design tells other animals, "Stay away, I'm poisonous!"

Shapes are important to plants, too. This plant shows a complex shape called a *fractal*. Don't know what a fractal is? Keep reading to find out!

Just like flying baseballs and flying cannonballs, rainbows are in the shape of a *parabola*. Unlike them, you will never see where a rainbow "lands"!

Shapes in nature

Animals using math

Though animals don't know the mathematical concepts behind some of their constructions, they do make things that take advantage of math. Let's see what some of our animal friends can make!

Pretty cool, huh?

DID YOU KNOW?

Wombat poop is shaped like a *cube!*

Bees get their food from flowers. They fly from flower to flower to drink a sweet juice called nectar, which they use to make honey. The bees deposit the nectar in a honeycomb, which is made of six-sided cells. These hexagonal cells **tesselate** and are an **efficient** use of space.

Spiders spin webs so that they can catch insects to eat. Many spiders build their webs in a spiral shape. This shape allows the spider to build as big a web as possible in a minimum amount of time. By the way, did you know that pound-for-pound, spider silk is five times stronger than steel?

If you have melissophobia (fear of bees), arachnophobia (fear of spiders), or ornithophobia (fear of birds), don't worry! The creatures on these pages are harmless ... and want to help you learn.

Many birds build their nests in a circular basket. One benefit of having a circular nest is that the birds can build a nest with the maximum *area* for the amount of twigs and other material they collect.

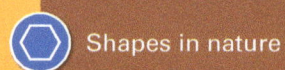
Shapes in nature

Stripes and spots

Zebras are animals that look like horses with stripes. These stripes are thought to provide *camouflage*, especially at night and in dim light. The stripes also help repel biting flies by disorienting their vision. Stripes also make it difficult for lions, cheetahs, and other animals that like to hunt zebras to single out individual zebras in a herd. Did you know that no two zebras have the same *pattern* of stripes?

Cheetahs have yellowish-brown fur with black spots. Like zebras, no two cheetahs have the same pattern of spots. These spots help cheetahs blend into their surroundings while hunting prey (such as zebras).

Cheetahs can run faster than any other land animal!

Don't tell the zebras that I am hiding here!

Many animals have colorful *shapes* on their bodies. Some of these *shapes* help them to eat ... or avoid being eaten!

Like cheetahs, ladybugs have spots. Unlike cheetahs, ladybugs don't use their spots to help them hunt zebras. Their spots serve as a "Don't eat me!" sign that tells hungry birds and other animals that the ladybugs don't taste good.

CURIOUS CONNECTIONS

PALEONTOLOGY In the movie *Jurassic World*, the fictional dinosaur *Indominus rex* had the ability to camouflage itself. Scientists believe that an actual dinosaur, *Psittacosaurus*, did have a type of camouflage. Neat trick, huh?

Psittacosaurus

Peacocks also have spots on their feathers. Male peacocks use these spotted feathers to help attract a mate.

 Shapes in nature

Elaborate **patterns**

In the real world, you may see these patterns in such things as beautiful mosaics or the skin of a snake.

The *shapes* that you are used to can be combined to make some cool-looking *patterns*. We can also combine shapes to make some awesome-looking designs that you have probably never seen before!

One advanced shape that you may not be familiar with is the *fractal*. Fractals are complex figures made up of patterns that repeat themselves at smaller and smaller scales. Fractals can form really interesting designs. One example is called the *Sierpiński* triangle:

Notice how in each black triangle a white triangle is drawn. You could (theoretically) do this forever and make an elaborate design. You could even make a 3D version of this triangle.

OK, so fractals make awesome-looking designs. But, where can they be seen in real life? Keep on reading to find out!

23

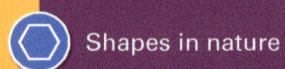 Shapes in nature

Triangular trees and fractal ferns

Evergreen trees have a triangular shape. This shape has many benefits. The top branches don't shade the lower branches, allowing all the branches to get sunlight. The shape also helps reduce wind resistance so that the wind can't easily knock over the tree.

In winter time, the shape of evergreen trees helps makes sure that snow doesn't collect on the top of the trees and knock them over.

Did you know that *shapes* matter to plants?

Let's see how the plant world uses shapes to its benefit. And, some of those cool-looking *fractals* we mentioned earlier!

Fractals are seen in the fern. Growing out of the stalk of the branch are leaflets that have the same shape as the branch. Each leaflet, in turn, is made up of smaller leaflets that also have the same shape as the branch.

The leaves of the aloe plant spiral out in a fractal pattern.

Fractals are also seen in the Romanesco cauliflower where the whole head of the cauliflower is made up of smaller heads (which, in turn, are made up of even smaller heads) that all resemble each other.

CAREER CORNER

If you enjoy plants, you may want to consider becoming a botanist! Botanists are scientists who study all aspects of plant life, including where they live and how they grow.

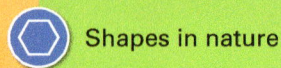

Shapes in nature

Rainbows

A rainbow is produced when raindrops are illuminated by sunlight. To see a rainbow, the sun must be behind you and the rain in front of you. If you are lucky, you might see a double rainbow. A double rainbow is caused when sunlight is reflected twice within a raindrop.

Here's a cool fact! No two people see the same rainbow! You are at center of the rainbow you see. This also means that you can never get to the end of a rainbow (and find a pot of gold!), because the rainbow moves with you.

Another fact that might surprise you about rainbows is that they are actually full circles! We only see a parabola because the rest of the rainbow is blocked by the ground. To see a full circle rainbow, you must be up high in the sky, for example in an airplane or helicopter.

A rainbow is a curved band of colored light that appears in the sky. Rainbows usually appear as a special type of curve called a *parabola*.

When you see a rainbow, the colors are always in the same order: red, orange, yellow, green, blue, indigo, and violet. Many people remember this order by using the acronym Roy G. Biv.

Red
Orange
Yellow
Green
Blue
Indigo
Violet

CURIOUS CONNECTIONS

PHYSICS You can use a triangular *prism* to make your own rainbow. Light, such as sunlight, contains all the colors of the rainbow mixed together. To show these colors, a beam of light is aimed so that it shines on a prism at a slant. As the beam enters the glass, it is refracted, or bent. But each color bends a different amount. As a result, when the light comes out of the prism, it is a band of colors like a rainbow.

SHAPES IN STRUCTURES

You can go to Egypt and see pyramids that are so old that King Tut would have called them ancient! In Greece you can visit the same buildings that Aristotle and Plato walked in! In Rome you can see aqueducts that may have brought water to Julius Caesar! In China you can walk over a bridge that was built before the Tang dynasty began!

This structure was built thousands of years ago! How can it still stand today? Much of the reason is due to the building's shape and the math behind it.

Travel with us across the globe as we see ancient and modern builders using different *shapes* to build amazing structures! Different shapes help keep structures standing....sometimes for centuries, or even millennia!

It's not just ancient societies that used math and shapes in their construction. Even today, people use circles, rectangles, and triangles when they are designing and building bridges, houses, skyscrapers, and many other structures.

Göbekli Tepe, a prehistoric site in Turkey, is believed to be the oldest known building that still exists. Construction of this temple began around 9000 B.C.

Shapes in structures

Build like an Egyptian

The Great Pyramid is heavy—it weighs about 6 million tons! Each side of the pyramid is built at an angle. Because of the angle, most of the pyramid's weight is in the lower half of the structure. Having less weight at the top allowed the pyramid to be built so high.

Before building the Great Pyramid, the Egyptians built what is known as the Bent Pyramid. See how the pyramid was originally built at one angle, and then about half-way up was built at a different angle? Many people believe that the Egyptians changed the angle to prevent the pyramid from becoming too heavy at the top and collapsing.

If you visit Egypt, you will see many pyramids. The largest pyramid ever built was the Great Pyramid of Giza. See how math has kept this pyramid (and others like it) standing for thousands of years!

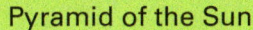

Pyramid of the Sun

The Egyptians weren't the only people to build pyramids. The ancient Maya built Chichén Itzá, and the ancient Aztec built the Pyramid of the Sun. Both pyramids are in Mexico. All four sides on Chichén Itzá have 91 steps, plus an additional step to access the temple. Why? Because 91 + 91 + 91 + 91 + 1 = 365, the number of days in a year!

Chichén Itzá

DID YOU KNOW?

The Great Pyramid was the world's largest structure for nearly 4,000 years! The pyramid was built about 2500 B.C. and remained the world's largest structure until the Lincoln Cathedral was built in London in A.D. 1311.

Shapes in structures

Ancient architecture

The *cylinder* is a strong shape to use in building. Many buildings have columns that are shaped like cylinders. Because cylinders don't have edges, their load is distributed throughout the column and not concentrated at the edges. The Parthenon, built about 2,500 years ago in ancient Greece, has 46 outside columns.

The **Great Wall of China**, the longest structure ever built, took centuries to build. Most of what is now called the Great Wall dates from the Ming dynasty (1368-1644). By the way, contrary to what you might have heard, you cannot see the Great Wall from the moon. It can only be seen from space in low *orbit* and under favorable conditions.

Math is not just for pyramids! In addition to the ancient Aztec, Egyptians, and Maya, other ancient civilizations also used the properties of *shapes* when building various structures.

Do you see the arches in this gateway and bridges in Foshan, China?

Keystone

Another strong shape is the *arch*, which has a semicircular shape. When an arch is built, the last block that is put in the arch is called the keystone. The keystone sits in the middle, between the two sides of the arch. Each side of the arch presses against the keystone. Because the weight is carried along the curve, the arch can support a lot of weight.

The Anji Bridge, in China, was built over 1,400 years ago.

The ancient Romans used arches to build bridges and aqueducts. Many Roman aqueducts, built about 2,000 years ago, are still standing today!

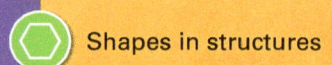
Shapes in structures

The mighty triangle!

Truss bridges are supported by frameworks made by triangles. Why triangles? Because objects made of triangles are much stronger than the usual strength of the materials from which they are made. This allows the bridge to be strong (and lighter, because it requires fewer materials). Truss bridges can, therefore, not only hold their own weight, but also the weight of the vehicles on them.

The Waibaidu Bridge in Shanghai, built over 100 years ago (!), was the first steel bridge built in China.

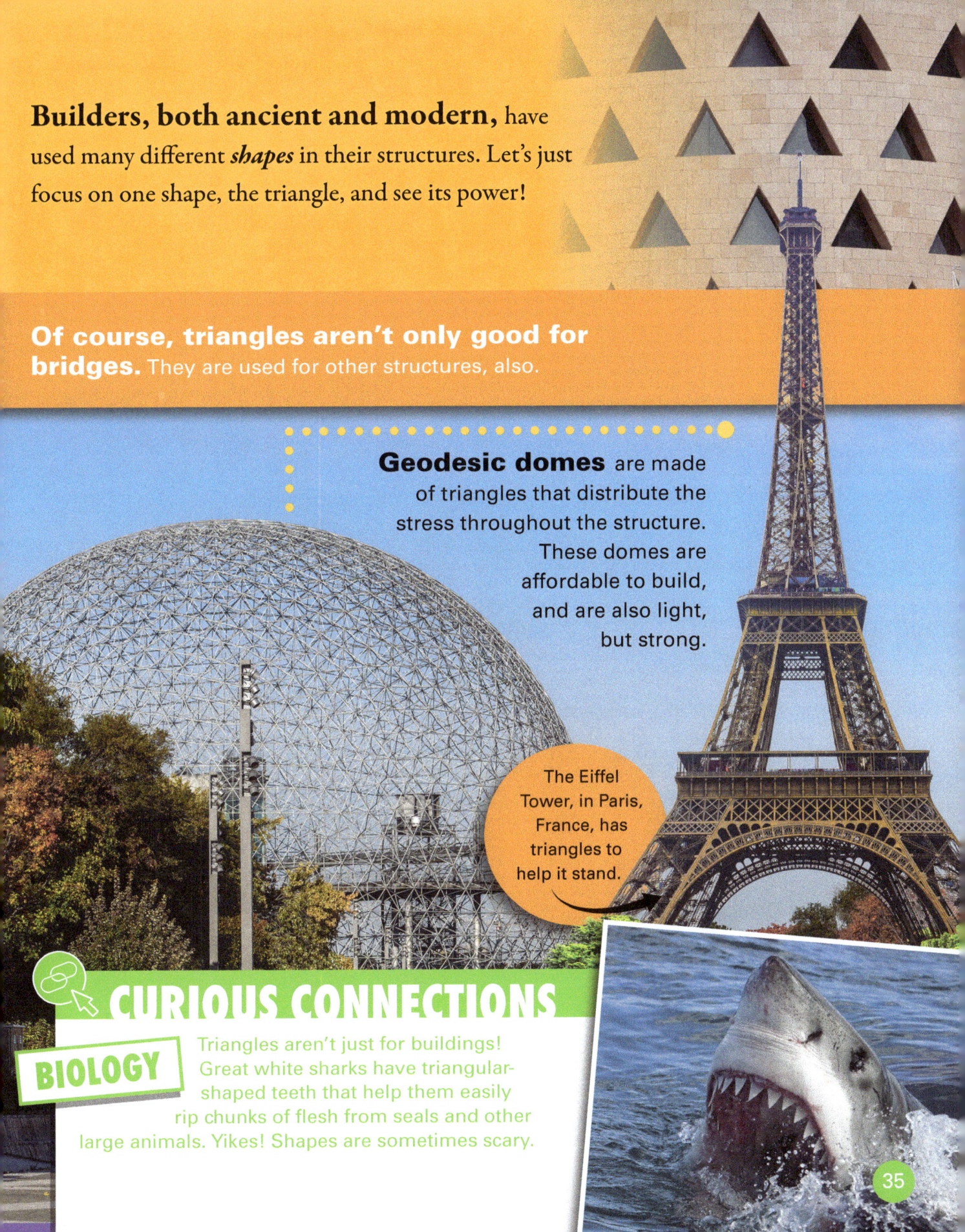

Builders, both ancient and modern, have used many different *shapes* in their structures. Let's just focus on one shape, the triangle, and see its power!

Of course, triangles aren't only good for bridges. They are used for other structures, also.

Geodesic domes are made of triangles that distribute the stress throughout the structure. These domes are affordable to build, and are also light, but strong.

The Eiffel Tower, in Paris, France, has triangles to help it stand.

CURIOUS CONNECTIONS

BIOLOGY Triangles aren't just for buildings! Great white sharks have triangular-shaped teeth that help them easily rip chunks of flesh from seals and other large animals. Yikes! Shapes are sometimes scary.

Shapes in structures

Contemporary construction

The Flatiron Building (built in New York City in 1902) is triangular. It was built this way to fit in the plot.

Most buildings are rectangular in shape. These buildings are easier and faster to make, more economical to build, and have less unused space than buildings of different shapes, such as the other ones on these two pages.

Some houses and buildings are round. These buildings are more energy *efficient*, more earthquake- and wind-resistant, and take less material to build.

The Marina City Towers (built in Chicago in 1967) are circular. Some Chicagoans think the towers look like corn cobs. What do you think?

Before triangles get too arrogant, we should note that architects have many *shapes* to choose from! Circles, rectangles, triangles, and other shapes are used in buildings around the world.

While flat roofs are cheaper to install, most houses have triangular roofs. These roofs allow rain to fall away from the house and help eliminate heavy snow build-up.

If you want to see Leonardo da Vinci's famous *Mona Lisa* painting, you must first visit a pyramid. Huh? A glass pyramid serves as the main entrance to the Louvre art museum in Paris.

CAREER CORNER

Architects use math to design buildings, find volumes and *areas*, and make accurate drawings that construction workers can use to build the buildings. Architects not only use math to make sure buildings stay up, but they also use geometry and *patterns* for design.

④ SHAPES IN SPACE

The universe is filled with all sorts of celestial bodies, such as stars, planets, moons, asteroids, and comets. And these celestial bodies might, at first glance, seem to be strangely shaped objects moving in random, chaotic ways. But, that isn't the case!

Even if we escape Earth, we can't escape the importance of math! We have seen math used on Earth; now it is time to see how math is used in space!

You probably take it for granted that everyone knows that Earth travels around the sun. But, that wasn't always the case! In the early 1500's, **Nicolaus Copernicus**, a Polish astronomer, explained that Earth traveled around the sun. In Copernicus's time, most astronomers believed that the sun traveled around Earth.

The *shapes* that we are learning about are not just for Earth-bound objects. Even in outer space, shapes (and the math behind them) play a role in what celestial bodies look like and how they move.

If you are reading this book, then you are currently in the Milky Way galaxy. (Either that, or this book has really travelled far!) Note the beautiful spiral *shape* of your home galaxy. In case you are wondering, you are on one of the spirals, not in the middle.

We might even correct some misconceptions that you have. You might think Earth is a perfectly round ball that travels in a perfect circle around the sun. As you will see, both statements are actually incorrect!

So, let's explore our universe and see more shapes in action.

Shapes in space

Ducks in space?

When you see a star (such as the sun), a planet (such as Earth), or a moon (well, such as the moon), you probably notice that all of them are basically spherical in *shape*. Do you think all objects in space are *spherical*? Actually, they are not!

Many asteroids, comets, and other space objects have strange *shapes*.

The asteroid Psyche looks like a potato

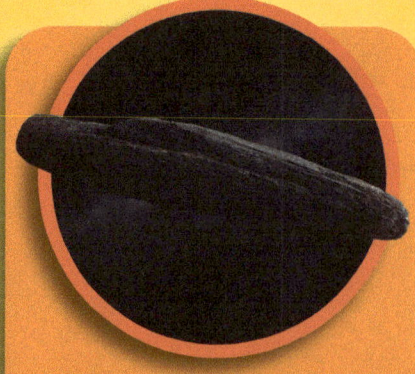

'Oumuamua, another space object, looks like a pencil.

Comet 67P/Churyumov-Gerasimenko looks like a rubber duck!

Have you ever used a telescope to look out into space? With a powerful enough telescope, you might see many spherical-shaped objects in space... and, possibly, a rubber ducky!

So why are there no strangely shaped planets (or stars or moons)? Because as gravity pulls equally from all sides, it works to make larger objects as compact as possible. So, in a big enough object, gravity will compact it into a *sphere*, a shape that has the least amount of surface *area*. Asteroids and comets are too small to have their shape affected by gravity.

DID YOU KNOW?

Earth (and the other planets in our solar system) are not perfect spheres. They are actually oblate spheroids. *Oblate spheroids* are kind of like spheres that have been squashed. Earth's spin causes the planet to bulge slightly at the equator.

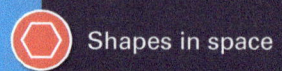
Shapes in space

Planets on the move

Earth and other planets don't *orbit* the sun in a perfect circle. They orbit the sun in an oval-shaped figure called an *ellipse*. Because of the *shape* of the orbit, Earth is not always the same distance from the sun.

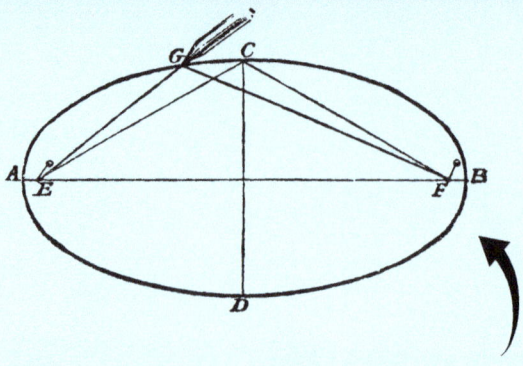

Ellipses are figures with the shape of a flattened hoop. To draw an ellipse, fasten the ends of a string at two points. Hold a pencil upright against the string so that the string is stretched tight at all times.

If you live in the Northern Hemisphere, you probably think that Earth is closest to the sun in summer, when it is hotter outside. Actually, Earth is closest to the sun in January and February when it is winter in the Northern Hemisphere.

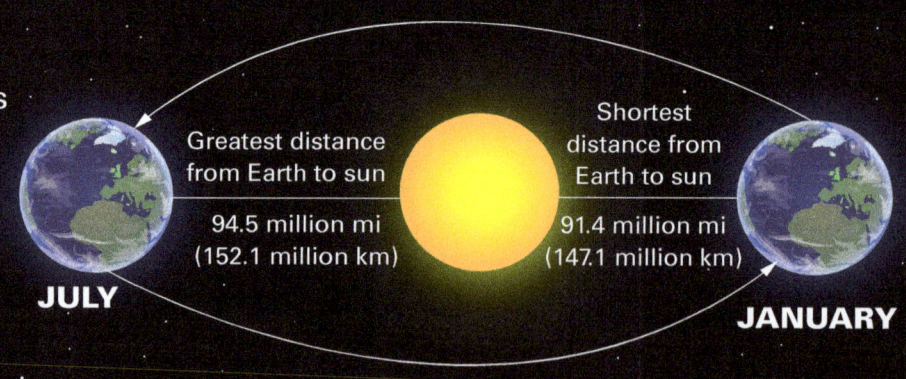

JULY — Greatest distance from Earth to sun 94.5 million mi (152.1 million km)

JANUARY — Shortest distance from Earth to sun 91.4 million mi (147.1 million km)

TECH TIME

Sending out space probes takes a lot of planning! Astronomers need to know the *shape* of planet orbits if they want to send a probe to explore them. For example, it takes several years for a probe to reach Jupiter. So, you don't send a probe to where Jupiter is now, but to where Jupiter will be several years from now when the probe arrives.

Quick question. True or false? All the planets in the solar system (including Earth) orbit the sun in a perfect circle. False! Read on to see why!

The moon orbits Earth in an ellipse.

It's not just planets that follow elliptical orbits. In fact, there are no known cases where one object in space orbits another in a perfect circle.

Halley's comet orbits the sun in a long, elliptical path.

Saturn's rings are made up mostly of pieces of ice. The individual pieces orbit the planet in an elliptical (although, almost circular) orbit.

Ellipses aren't only seen in orbits. Jupiter's Great Red Spot is an ellipse (well, mostly). The spot has a bigger circumference than Earth has! The spot is a swirling cloud of gas that rotates around the planet.

The power of the cylinder!

You will need:
- Construction paper (or, preferably, thick pieces of paper)
- Scotch tape
- Books that are the same weight (preferably ones that aren't too heavy)
- Ruler
- Pencil

Give it a try

1. Take one piece of paper and turn it horizontally. Using a ruler and pencil, divide it into four equal parts. Fold along the lines and make a rectangular prism. Tape the sides so that the prism stays together.
2. Take another piece of paper and divide it into three equal parts horizontally. Fold along the lines and make a triangular prism. Tape the sides so that the prism stays together.
3. Take the third piece of paper and roll it into a cylinder and tape it together.

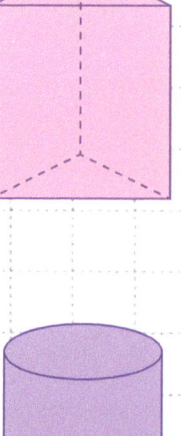

There's a reason we trust *cylinders* to support structures and protect grocery store products. It's because they're a strong and powerful *shape*. Put this shape to the test! Will the cylinder live up to its reputation? Or, will it collapse under the pressure?

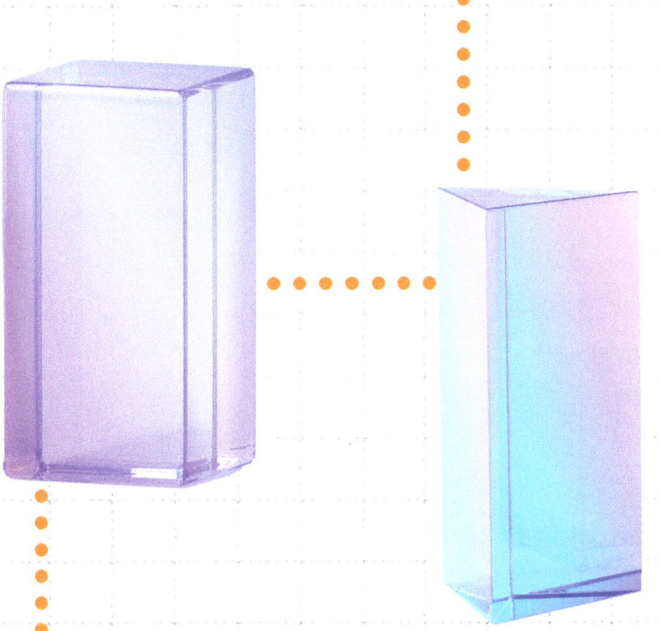

4. Make a chart to record how many books each of the three shapes can hold.

Shape	Number of books
Triangular prism	
Rectangular prism	
Cylinder	

5. Stack books on each shape one at a time. Keep stacking until the shape collapses. For each shape, record the number of books that you stacked before the collapse.

Try this next!

You can extend this activity by making three or four of each shape and seeing how many books you can stack on them. Do you think the same shape that held up the most books with only one piece of paper will hold up the most with three or four? Make a prediction and write it down. What were the results? Were they what you expected?

QUESTION TIME!

Look at your results. Which shape held up the most books? Was there a big difference in the number of books the shapes held?

Index

A
animals, 16-21
Anji Bridge (China), 33
aqueducts, 28, 32
arches, 32-33
architecture, 32-33, 37
area, 10, 19, 37, 41
Aztec, 31

B
biology, 35
board games, 14-15
botany, 25
bridges, 28-29, 32-34

C
camouflage, 20-21
chess, 14-15
circles, 10-11, 19, 27, 29, 32, 37
Copernicus, Nicolaus, 39
cubes, 13, 19
cylinders, 12, 32, 44-45

D
dimensions, 15

E
Earth (as an object in space), 11, 39-43
efficiency, 18, 36
Eiffel Tower (France), 35
ellipses, 11, 42-43

F
Flatiron Building (New York City), 37
fractals, 17, 22-25

G
geodesic domes, 35
Giant's Causeway (Northern Ireland), 8
Go (board game), 15
Göbekli Tepe (Turkey), 29
gravity, 41
Great Pyramid of Giza (Egypt), 30-31
Great Wall of China, 33
great white sharks, 35
Guangzhou Circle (China), 11

H
hexagons, 8-9, 18

I
intersections, 15

J
Jupiter, 43

K
keystones, 32
kites, 8-9

M
Marina City Towers (Chicago), 37

Maya, 31
Milky Way galaxy, 39
moon (of Earth), 40, 43

O
oblate spheroids, 41
orbits, 11, 33, 42-43
'Oumuamua (space object), 40
outer space, 33, 38-43

P
paleontology, 21
parabolas, 11, 17, 27
parallelograms, 8-9
Parthenon (Greece), 12, 32
patterns, 20-25, 37
pentagons, 8-9
physics, 27
plants, 17, 24-25
polygons, 8-9
prisms, 13, 27, 44-45
Psittacosaurus (dinosaur), 21
Psyche (asteroid), 40
pyramids, 28, 30-31, 37

Q
quadrilaterals, 8-9

R
rainbows, 17, 26-27
rectangles, 8-9, 13, 29, 36-37, 44-45
rhombuses, 8-9

S
Saturn, 43
Sierpiński triangles, 22-23
space probes, 43
spheres, 41
spirals, 18, 25, 39
square numbers, 14-15
square roots, 15
squares, 8-9, 14-15
sun, 11, 26, 39-40, 42-43

T
tessellation, 18
trapezoids, 8-9
triangles, 8, 22-24, 27, 29, 34-37, 44-45

W
Waibaidu Bridge (China), 34

Glossary

arch (ahrch)—a curved structure capable of bearing the weight of the material above it

area (AIR ee uh)—the space inside a flat shape

camouflage (KAM uh flahzh)—a disguise or false appearance in order to conceal; protective coloration

cube (kyoob)—a solid shape with six square faces or sides, all equal

cylinder (SIHL uhn duhr)—a solid shape; its ends are two equal circles

dimension (duh MEHN shuhn)—a measurement of length, breadth, or thickness

efficient (uh FIHSH uhnt)—able to produce the effect wanted without waste of time or energy

ellipse (ih LIHPS)—an oval shaped like a flattened hoop

fractal (FRAK tuhl)—geometric shapes in which similar patterns appear at even-smaller scales

intersection (IHN tuhr SEHK shuhn)—the point or line where one thing crosses another

kite (kyt)—a flat, four-sided plane figure with two pairs of adjacent congruent sides

orbit (AWR biht)—the path of Earth or any one of the planets around the sun

parabola (puh RAB uh luh)—a curve like the path of a ball batted high in the air

parallelogram (PAR uh LEHL uh gram)—a flat, four-sided plane figure whose opposite sides are parallel and equal

pattern (PAT uhrn)—an arrangement of forms and colors; design

polygon (POL ee gon)—a closed plane figure having three or more angles and straight sides

prism (PRIHZ uhm)—a solid with two parallel bases joined by three or more sides

rhombus (ROM buhs)—a parallelogram with equal sides, usually having two obtuse angles and two acute angles

shape (shayp)—the outward outline of an object; form; figure

sphere (sfihr)—a perfectly round solid shape

square number—the product of a number multiplied by itself

square root—a number that produces a given number when multiplied by itself

tesselate (tess eh layt)—to make a pattern of interlocking shapes leaving no spaces or overlaps

trapezoid (TRAP uh zoyd)—a four-sided plane figure having two sides parallel and sides not parallel

www.ingramcontent.com/pod-product-compliance
Lightning Source LLC
Chambersburg PA
CBHW061250170426

43191CB00041B/2410